Ancient Egyptian War and Weapons

Brenda Williams

Heinemann
LIBRARY

www.heinemann.co.uk/library
Visit our website to find out more information about **Heinemann Library** books.

To order:
☎ Phone 44 (0) 1865 888066
▤ Send a fax to 44 (0) 1865 314091
▢ Visit the Heinemann Bookshop at www.heinemann.co.uk/library to browse our catalogue and order online.

First published in Great Britain by Heinemann Library, Halley Court, Jordan Hill, Oxford OX2 8EJ, part of Harcourt Education Ltd. Heinemann is a registered trademark of Harcourt Education Ltd.

Editorial: Nick Hunter and Jennifer Tubbs
Design: Jo Hinton-Malivoire and Tinstar Design (www.tinstar.co.uk)
Illustrations: Art Construction
Picture Research: Maria Joannou and Virginia Stroud-Lewis
Production: Viv Hichens

Originated by Ambassador Litho Ltd
Printed in Hong Kong, China by Wing King Tong

ISBN 0 431 14580 6
06 05 04 03 02
10 9 8 7 6 5 4 3 2 1

British Library Cataloguing in Publication Data
Williams, Brenda
    Ancient Egyptian War and Weapons.
    – (People in the Past)
    355'.02'0932

Acknowledgements
The publishers would like to thank the following for permission to reproduce photographs:
AKG London pp. **5**, **36**, **43**; Ancient Art and Architecture Collection pp. **8**, **20**, **22**, **30**, **32**, **38**, **40**; Ancient Egypt Picture Library pp. **7**, **17**, **19**, /Robert Partridge p. **24**; Philip Cooke/Magnet Harlequin pp. **18**, **42**; Corbis p. **26**; Corbis/Sandro Vannini p. **23**; Peter Evans p. **34**; Michael Holford p. **16**; Photo Archive p. **13**; Scala Art Collection p. **14**; Werner Forman Archive pp. **6**, **9**, **11**, **15**, **28**.

Cover photograph of model soldiers from an ancient-Egyptian tomb reproduced with permission of Photo Archive.

The publishers would like to thank Dr Christina Riggs for her assistance in the preparation of this book.

Every effort has been made to contact copyright holders of any material reproduced in this book. Any omissions will be rectified in subsequent printings if notice is given to the publishers.

Contents

Words appearing in the text in bold, **like this**, are explained in the Glossary.

Who were the ancient Egyptians?

The Egyptians created the first great **civilization** of the ancient world, a remarkable way of life that lasted for about 3000 years. The Egyptians were ruled by kings, all-powerful rulers who in the New Kingdom (from about 1539 BC) were known as pharaohs. Many of these pharaohs were conquerors, leading armies of warriors into battle. Yet the Egyptians were less warlike than their enemies, such as the Assyrians and **Hittites**, who lived in what are now Iraq and Turkey. Most Egyptians were farmers, living in a fruitful, green land between harsh deserts. Egypt's warriors went to war to protect their land, and to add new territory and riches to their **empire**.

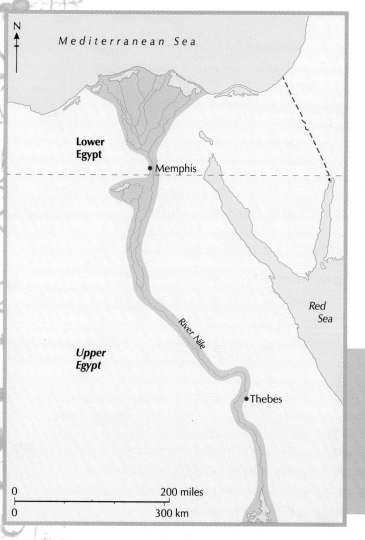

The land of Egypt

Most of Egypt's land was hot and dry, as it still is today. Through the sun-scorched desert ran a narrow strip of green fields and trees watered by the River Nile, flowing north from the heart of Africa. Every year the Nile flooded as water from distant mountains flowed north to the sea. The rising waters spread black fertile soil along the riverbank, nourishing the fields where farmers grew food. People settled along the Nile, building temples and cities.

This map shows Upper and Lower Egypt, and the River Nile flowing to the sea. Conquered or weaker rulers were expected to send gifts, called **tribute**, to Egypt's king. In its long history, Egypt had several capital cities, including Memphis and Thebes.

This **relief** carving in stone shows a sea battle that took place in the 11th century BC. With their round shields, the enemy are trying to fend off arrows fired at them by Egyptian **archers**.

How do we know?

The Egyptians left some of the most amazing **monuments** in the world. Visitors to Egypt still marvel at the ancient stone temples, the mighty pyramids and the tombs in the Valley of the Kings, where the Egyptians buried their rulers. The most famous tomb is that of the boy-pharaoh Tutankhamen, who ruled from 1333 BC to 1323 BC. The tomb contained treasures and everyday things, including armour and weapons, that had been buried with the young king.

A priest named Manetho, who lived in the 200s BC, wrote a history of Egypt. He named 30 **dynasties**, or families of pharaohs. Other evidence comes from picture writing or **hieroglyphs**, written on the walls of temples and tombs, and on sheets of **papyrus**. From these writings, historians have worked out that about 5000 years ago, a warrior-leader named Menes from southern or Upper Egypt conquered Lower Egypt, so called because it was closer to the mouth of the Nile and the sea. Menes united Egypt, which grew to be the first 'super-power' in history.

In this book, you will discover how Egypt's warriors were trained, and what weapons they used. You will also learn how they fought battles on land and sea against enemies greedy to seize Egypt's wealth. Throughout its long history, Egypt's soldiers (who included people from many lands) built forts and fought battles to defend this mighty civilization, whose remains still inspire awe in us today.

The first armies

The first people to live along the banks of the River Nile were farmers and hunters. They fought with stone knives and clubs, and the soldier with the heaviest club usually won. Evidence for these weapons comes from shallow pit-graves, which contain stone club-heads. Around 3400 BC, a Nile people known as Gerzeans were fighting with pear-shaped clubs called maces, heavy enough to break an opponent's arm, and so leave him helpless.

Warrior-pharaohs

One of Egypt's earliest **monuments**, from over 5000 years ago, shows a giant-sized pharaoh killing an enemy with a mace. Such pictures tell us that people admired a ruler strong enough to drive away enemies. Later, every Egyptian pharaoh was pictured as a soldier, even if he never actually fought a battle. Pictures in the tomb of Tutankhamen show the boy-pharaoh driving a **chariot**, but, so far as we know, he never actually went to war.

About 3000 BC, we have evidence of Egypt's first named pharaoh, Menes. He made himself ruler of all Egypt, choosing Memphis as his capital, with a **garrison** of soldiers and shipyards to build boats. The Egyptian army was small. The pharaoh had his own **bodyguard**, but called up part-time soldiers to fight in wars and go off on expeditions. Later pharaohs often paid foreign soldiers to fight for them, as **mercenaries**.

A picture cut into slate shows a pharaoh with a war club standing over a defeated enemy chief. The pharaoh is called Narmer, but some historians think that Narmer could be another name for Menes. He is probably killing the captive, to please the gods, such as the falcon-headed Horus (top right).

Military expeditions and officials

Pharaohs sent out expeditions beyond Egypt's borders. They sent boats down the Nile and parties of men with donkeys to carry loads across the desert. Soldiers guarded these trade missions, and also marched into the desert to escort gold-miners and slaves cutting stones for the royal palaces, pyramids and temples.

In Egypt, the pharaoh had complete power. Officials passed on his orders to junior officials, tax collectors and **scribes**. From tomb inscriptions and other writings, we know about some of these civil servants – for example, we know that Weni, an official serving the pharaoh Pepi I (about 2325 BC to about 2150 BC), recruited **Nubian** soldiers to strengthen the army. Weni also saw himself as a tactician (someone who made battle plans), telling soldiers they must attack first, not wait for an enemy to attack them! He had canals dug beside the Nile's first cataract, or rapids, so that troops in boats could by-pass the wild waters safely.

Sacrifices to the gods

After Menes defeated the rulers of northern Egypt, he celebrated by **sacrificing** ten captives as thanks offerings to the gods. A picture shows the captives with their heads cut off. Sacrificing captives became an Egyptian custom, though some Egyptians thought it cruel and 'barbaric'. Royal captives were sometimes spared, if valuable as **hostages**.

Prehistoric Egyptian weapons included this stone mace head. At the base of the head the hole for a wooden handle can be seen. Gripping the handle, a warrior tried to hit enemy soldiers with the hard stone. It could bruise and break bones.

Metal weapons

Ancient peoples made stone clubs, axes and knives. By 4000 BC, the Egyptians had found out how to make weapons from **copper**, a metal that is soft enough to be hammered into shape without being heated in a fire.

Making better weapons

The Egyptians became skilled in making copper tools and weapons, including spears, daggers (short, stabbing knives) and swords. They also made leather **helmets**, and leather and wooden **shields** for protection against metal weapons. Maces with sharper curved edges developed into battleaxes.

Copper is so soft, however, that soldiers often found their weapons snapped or bent during a battle. Seeking a tougher material, Egyptian metalworkers tried heating copper with other metal-bearing rocks. They found that by mixing eight parts of copper with one part of tin they could make **bronze**. Melted bronze could be poured into a sand, clay or stone mould and when the liquid metal cooled, it hardened to a useful shape. Using this method, the Egyptians made bronze swords, spearheads and axes. These were sharper and harder than copper weapons.

Spearheads were fixed to wooden shafts. Copper spears (right, 800 BC) broke and bent easily. Bronze (centre, 1300 BC) was harder. Harder still was iron (left), but the Egyptians did not use iron spears until around 600 BC.

Sesostris I is featured on this **relief**. Warrior pharaohs like this strong ruler recorded their campaigns in written inscriptions, for future generations to admire.

Local rulers and strong pharaohs

Tin was scarce in Egypt, so bronze was precious. Bronze weapons were not made until after 2000 BC, around the end of the Old Kingdom. During this period of Egyptian history the pharaohs lost power to local rulers, called **nomarchs**, who led their own armies.

A strong pharaoh named Amenemhet I seized the throne in 1938 BC. His son Sesostris I ruled with him, and for ten years the two of them fought the southern **Nubians**, and northern enemies in Syria and Palestine. While Sesostris was away fighting in Libya, his father Amenemhet was murdered (probably by a rival). Sesostris must have had the army on his side, because he came out on top and ruled Egypt for over 30 years. Under these strong rulers, power in Egypt swung back to the pharaoh, the leader of conquering armies.

Showing the flag

Pharaohs sent out military expeditions to scare off raiding **nomads**, such as **Bedouins**, and to remind local rulers of the pharaoh's power. Captives and **slaves** built forts, from which soldiers could control trade and travel along the Nile. Sesostris III (1836 BC to 1818 BC) built a chain of forts from Buhen to Semna. He reduced the power of the **nobles** further, by dividing Egypt into four districts under central control. Citizen-soldiers were conscripted from every district by royal command.

Invaders with new weapons

By around 1600 BC, Egypt had again grown weak. In the south the Egyptians lost control of **Nubia** and its **garrisons** were taken over by Nubians. More dangerous still, from the north, people the Egyptians called 'Asiatics' began to invade from Syria and Palestine, and settle in the Nile Delta.

The Hyksos take over

The 'Asiatics' took control of Lower Egypt, starting their own line of pharaohs (the 15th **Dynasty**), and ruling from their city of Avaris. The Egyptians called these new rulers Hyksos, a name which probably meant 'rulers of a foreign country' (it was once thought to mean 'shepherd kings'). The newcomers copied many Egyptian ways, but they had nothing to learn about warfare. Their weapons were better than any the Egyptians had.

The Hyksos wore body armour made of leather and metal, while the Egyptians fought practically naked apart from a short **kilt**. Their wooden, skin-covered **shields** gave little protection against the Hyksos soldiers, slashing with razor-sharp curved swords. Hyksos **archers** shot arrows from **composite** bows. They could hit a man at 400 metres, twice as far as an Egyptian archer shooting a simple wooden bow.

Chariot attack

Most frightening of all, the Hyksos charged into action in **chariots**, pulled by horses. This was a weapon totally new to Egypt's foot soldiers. Each chariot carried an archer or a spearman, as well as a driver.

The gods of Egypt

The Egyptians had many gods. The chief gods were the sun god Re (or Ra), Osiris, god of death and nature, his wife Isis and their son Horus. Though most of Egypt's gods were peaceful, there were war-gods, such as Sekhmet, a woman with the head of a lioness and Mont or Mentu, who cut off the heads of the pharaohs' enemies with his sword. The desert god Seth was feared as the bringer of storm and destruction.

The Egyptians were beaten by the better armed Hyksos armies, but quickly learned to use these new weapons themselves. Around 1540 BC, the 17th Dynasty Pharaoh Kamose led the fight back, from his own chariot. When Kamose died, possibly from wounds suffered in battle, his brother Ahmose I (about 1539 BC to 1514 BC) became pharaoh in his place.

The New Kingdom

Ahmose too was a soldier-king and reunited Egypt, driving the Hyksos back into Palestine. He rewarded his soldiers with treasure and with captives to keep as **slaves**. His officers became a new special military class who served the pharaoh and led the army to defend the New Kingdom of Egypt.

The war-goddess Sekhmet. Egyptians believed the kindly goddess Hathor changed into a lioness to punish humans for rebelling against the sun god Re. She became the terrible Sekhmet. Statues of the gods were carried with marching armies.

The new army

Until about 1500 BC, the Egyptians did not feel the need for a large full-time army. Then when the New Kingdom began, the country went 'soldier-crazy'. Tomb inscriptions from this date boast of the bravery of Egypt's soldiers, while pictures show the pharaoh as a god-like warrior, riding in his **chariot**.

Ahmose's good advice to Amenhotep

Ahmose I (ruled from about 1539 BC to 1514 BC), vanquisher of the Hyksos, was the model for these new hero-pharaohs. Leaving his mother Ahhotep to rule in Thebes, he led a river fleet to attack Avaris and chased the Hyksos north into Palestine, where he laid **siege** to their stronghold of Sharuhen for three years.

Ahmose taught his son, Amenhotep I, that a pharaoh must attend to every detail. When the young prince wanted to dash off in his chariot, the pharaoh told him to 'first make sure the shipyards at Memphis have enough timber to repair and build your ships'.

Wood was scarce in Egypt, and the best timber (wood used for building) had to be imported. Ahmose also advised that a wise king would reopen disused **copper** mines, so that the soldiers could have new weapons, and rebuild the desert forts to defend the mines and Egypt's frontiers.

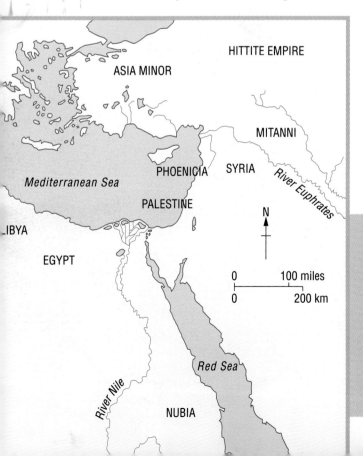

HITTITE EMPIRE

ASIA MINOR

MITANNI

PHOENICIA   SYRIA   River Euphrates

Mediterranean Sea

PALESTINE

N

LIBYA

EGYPT

0   100 miles
0   200 km

Red Sea

River Nile

NUBIA

Egypt needed its army to fight many enemies. These enemies included **Bedouin** nomads, Libyans from the desert, and the **Nubians** in the south. To the north and east lived powerful peoples such as the **Hittites**, Mitannians, Canaanites, Syrians and Phoenicians. The **Sea Peoples** attacked Egypt from the Mediterranean Sea.

Rewarded for running the army

Amenhotep, son of Hapu (about 1460 BC to 1380 BC), held the title of **Scribe** of the Recruits under Pharaoh Amenhotep III. His job was to make sure the army was up to strength. He did his job well. He set up new checkpoints along the Nile, where travellers were questioned. He sent out desert patrols to chase away **nomads**, who were trying to steal Egyptian sheep or cattle. The pharaoh gave him a funeral chamber next to the royal temple – a rare honour for a scribe.

Citizen-soldiers

Army officers now ran much of the government of Egypt, and called up small numbers of citizens from towns and villages to serve as soldiers. Other men volunteered for the army. The new recruits reported to their local commander for training. **Veteran** soldiers showed them how to throw a spear, shoot a bow and hold a **shield** properly. They kept fit by running and wrestling.

In return for army service, recruits were given weapons and food. After they had served their time, **conscripts** were free to go home for the harvest but were on standby to fight if their pharaoh needed them. Soldiers spent much of their time guarding forts and checkpoints along the River Nile. They looked forward to going home to their villages, to work on their farms and see their families.

These model soldiers were placed in the tomb of a district governor called Mesehti. He led troops in life, so when he died he was buried with soldiers to lead into the next world. The marching men carry spears and ox-hide shields.

The soldier's life

When looking for new recruits, an officer chose men with useful skills. Egyptians worked hard from childhood, usually outdoors in the fields, so the average soldier would have been good at digging, making mud-bricks and reed baskets. Some had other skills, such as making clay pots or wooden furniture.

The chances of fame and fortune

Most soldiers were young and fit. Many recruits would have enjoyed wrestling, a favourite sport in Egypt. Tomb pictures show wrestlers, with funny written captions such as, 'And now you'll find yourself flat on your face'. Local part-time soldiers took part in village war dances, organized by the district commander to boost 'team spirit'.

Many soldiers were volunteers who joined the army because they were poor and hoped to come home with **loot** and **slaves** captured from the enemy. If he escaped being killed or struck down by disease, a retired soldier hoped for a gift of land. Winning commanders were rewarded with slaves, loot and land, but in return had to send at least one son back into the army. An officer who impressed the pharaoh might end up as an important official. A lucky soldier might come home with a gold fly decoration, an award for bravery in battle.

A wall painting shows Egyptians wrestling. We know this was a favourite sport, and 'unarmed combat' was probably part of the soldier's training. On the battlefield, soldiers fought with whatever weapons they had, or none.

How the army was organized

When battle began, old soldiers stood in front of the inexperienced troops. The best soldiers were the special troops, known as 'The Braves'. Picked for their loyalty and bravery, they took on the most dangerous missions, such as climbing the walls of enemy towns and forts, raiding enemy camps and leading charges.

Each soldier lived with nine comrades, sharing food and making camp together. Five of these ten-man squads formed a 'Fifty', led by a junior officer. Four 'Fifties' made a company of 200 men, each with its own name and **standard**-bearer. The army's largest fighting units were divisions, named after gods. Each division had 5000 men, including 1000 **chariot** troops.

Clothes and kit

Soldiers travelled light. Egypt was hot, so men and women wore light, cool clothing. A soldier's **kilt** was made from **linen**. He wore sandals of **papyrus** reed. To save wear and tear, soldiers often wore leather aprons over their kilts. They shaved with **copper** or **bronze** razors and wore lucky charms (such as animal bones or small figures of gods) on a bracelet or necklace.

This is a preparatory drawing for a piece of art. A soldier could throw a spear like a javelin, or he could use it to stab at an enemy when fighting at close range.

15

Into battle

Models of Egyptian soldiers, found in tombs, show how lightly armed they were. They wore hardly any body armour, and only light cloth or leather helmets. Marching into battle, many soldiers must have been wounded by flying stones and arrows before they got close to the enemy. Egyptians relied on speed and sheer numbers to win their battles.

On the march, officers led the column of soldiers, followed by **standard**-bearers. Each company had its own standard, borne as proudly as the flags carried by soldiers today. Trumpeters marched alongside the column, blowing shrill calls to tell the soldiers what to do. Next came the **chariots**. Their wheels and the hooves of the horses, kicking up clouds of dust, must have choked the lines of foot-soldiers, or **infantry**, marching along behind.

Battle is joined

Before a battle, armies often made camp in sight of one another. They drew up in fighting formation at daybreak. To guard against surprise attacks, a wise commander sent out spies and **scouts** to report on the strength and position of the enemy.

A detail of a **relief** in Thebes. It shows Egyptian soldiers marching with their shields and long spears as they journey to a foreign land.

Trumpet calls

Trumpeters blew loud calls to give commands. The soldiers were trained to obey different calls, such as 'Advance' or 'Stand your ground'. Tomb pictures of battle scenes show trumpeters and standard-bearers leading attacks. On the march, the trumpeters blew short notes, to time the steps of the soldiers. Two fine war-trumpets were found in Tutankhamen's tomb. One was silver, the other was made of **bronze** covered with gold, so these trumpets were too good for battle use.

The Egyptians were used to fighting in the open desert. Battle began with a flurry of arrows, spears and stones hurled by **slingers**. Next, chariots would dash in to try and break up the lines of enemy foot soldiers, standing still behind their **shields**. If this worked, the infantry would charge into the scattering enemy, often in a favourite formation, a square. The serious fighting was hand-to-hand combat, with swords, clubs and axes. Battles must have been very noisy, with blaring trumpets, beating drums, shouts, screams and war cries.

Standards and flags

In the confusion, standards and flags were rallying points. Egyptian armies had flags like streamers, made from cloth. A strip of cloth blowing in the wind was useful to **archers**, to show them which way the wind was blowing. It could also easily be seen by soldiers. In battle, soldiers followed their standard – a tall pole with a small statue of a protecting god fixed to the top. Soldiers believed that carrying their gods into battle would bring them victory.

This trumpet found in Tutankhamen's tomb can still be played. The decoration shows the pharaoh with three gods.

Charging chariots

In Egypt, the donkey was more common than the horse. Donkeys were used to carry loads on their backs, and rich people rode in **litters** carried between donkeys. The Egyptians did not use camels until the time of Queen Cleopatra in the 1st century BC. Oxen, not horses, pulled ploughs and carts. Until late in their history, the Egyptians had no **cavalry**. Only one weapon relied on horses – the **chariot**, which carried pharaohs and nobles to war.

Chariot power

The chariot was a two-wheeled cart, carrying a driver and a warrior. It was normally pulled by two horses, harnessed by chest-straps either side of a long pole. The Egyptians learned about chariots the hard way, by fighting the Hyksos, who were the first enemies to send chariots thundering into battle against them. The Hyksos chariot charges must have terrified Egyptian soldiers, some of whom may never have seen a horse before.

The Egyptian chariot

The Egyptians learned fast, and soon built their own chariots. These were very light, with frames of thin wood covered by canvas. The floor was made of leather straps covered with a rug or animal skin. The wheels had six spokes, which made them very strong. The Egyptian chariot was fast, yet well balanced, so the driver could turn sharply without toppling the vehicle over.

Here is Ramses III (ruled 1187 BC to 1156 BC) in his chariot, firing his bow to scatter Egypt's enemies. This picture was carved on the wall of the pharaoh's great temple, to boast of his victories.

This is what a chariot looked like. Six chariots were found in the tomb of Tutankhamen for the pharaoh to use in the afterlife. On a box in Tutankhamen's tomb is a picture of him in a war chariot, though it is unlikely that he ever fought in a battle.

Chariots in battle

In each division of the Egyptian army, there were about 500 chariots which rode into battle in squadrons of 25. Each chariot carried two men, standing up. One man was the driver; the other was the fighter. The driver would charge towards the enemy soldiers at top speed, and then swerve sideways so that the warrior could fire arrows or throw spears. The driver sent the chariot speeding away in a shower of dust and stones.

Chariots were also used to defend the Egyptian **infantry** from enemy chariots, by driving in front of the marching men. Most of the chariot warriors were young **nobles**, who liked to show off by driving very fast, or dashing in close to the enemy. They practised shooting arrows while driving, lashing the reins around their waist to control the chariot. Such skill would be vital in battle if the chariot driver was killed or wounded.

Horses to war

Horses in Egypt were probably not big enough to be ridden into battle by heavily armed soldiers, though lightly clothed **scouts** probably galloped off on horseback to spy on the enemy. It took two small horses to pull a chariot. The trouble was that if one horse was injured, or a wheel came off, the chariot was out of action. In most armies, chariots were replaced by cavalry, mounted on stronger horses, by the 500s BC.

Axemen and archers

Three favourite weapons in Egypt were the club, the battleaxe and the bow. Soldiers usually became skilled with one or two weapons. **Archers** carried clubs, to use when all their arrows were gone. Axemen fought in groups, alongside companies of archers, spearmen and club-men.

Axes and clubs

Egyptian axes were simpler than those of their enemies. The battleaxe had a short wooden handle, to which was fastened a head made of stone, **copper** or **bronze**. The axe-head was at first lashed in place, by wedging it into the split wood and binding it tight with thongs. Later, the handle was forced through a hole in the axe-head, so it was less likely to fall off. Most axes had short blades, though some were long and curved.

To smash an enemy's head or arm, a soldier used a club or mace. This was made of stone or wood. Some clubs had ball-shaped heads and others were more egg-shaped.

Bows and arrows

Many Egyptians learned to shoot bows and arrows as children, hunting birds beside the Nile. Hunters were also skilled in flinging stones and sticks, so many soldiers had a strong throwing arm and a keen eye. At first, the Egyptian bow was a feeble weapon, which

Archers in the army of Ramses III at Medinet Habu, in western Thebes, Egypt. This shows Egyptian soldiers attacking an enemy with a volley of arrows. Battles were often started by the archers.

The archer-pharaoh's warning

Amenhotep II was pharaoh of Egypt from 1426 BC to 1400 BC. He loved to show off his skill as an archer and, when he died, he was buried with his bow. While fighting the Syrians, the pharaoh displayed his shooting in front of the town of Kadesh to frighten the townspeople. Coming home after victory with about 90,000 prisoners, he had the bodies of seven dead Syrian princes hung from the walls of cities in **Nubia**. The grim warning worked. The Nubians kept the peace – they saw what would happen if they did not.

could not fire arrows far enough to keep enemy soldiers at a distance. Things improved after the Egyptians began copying the **composite** bows of their Hyksos enemies.

The composite bow

The secret of the composite bow lay in its 'glued-strip' shape. The bow was made of layers of bark, animal sinew and horn glued over a long strip of springy wood forced into a curved shape. These layers made it very strong. As he drew the bowstring of twisted sinew, the archer pulled the curved tips of the bow backwards. It took great strength to bend the bow 'the wrong way', almost into a half-circle. When he let go, the arrow flew with tremendous force, up to 400 metres away.

Arrows and tactics

Arrows were made of reeds or strips of wood, tipped with a sharp point or head. Arrowheads were made first of stone, bone or hard ebony wood, and later from copper and bronze. Broad, hooked arrowheads tore a large and often fatal wound. Slim points went in further and usually killed the victim outright if they struck a vital organ.

Archers carried thirty arrows in a **quiver**. They wore leather bands to protect their wrists from the 'snap' of the bowstring when it was released. They also wore bone finger-guards. Archers fought at long range, firing arrows into the mass of enemy soldiers. When **chariots** attacked, the archers tried to bring down the horses.

Swords, spears and stones

All warriors in ancient times admired a good sword. It took time and skill to make a sword. The finest swords were usually princes' weapons.

Daggers and swords

Egyptian swords were first made of beaten **copper** and later of **bronze**. Iron swords were much stronger and less likely to snap in battle, but they were very rare before 1000 BC. An iron dagger found in Tutankhamen's tomb must have been a valuable treasure. Daggers, which were like short swords, were carried in the belt and used for self-defence.

Though longer than a dagger, the common Egyptian sword was still quite short. The soldier held it tightly, because he did not want the sword knocked from his hand during a fight. The short sword had a pointed tip, so was good for stabbing at an enemy.

The Egyptians also copied a curved sword, called a *khepesh*, from the Hyksos. This looked rather like the **sickle** that farmers used to cut ripe wheat. The swordsman slashed with it when fighting.

On this decorated shield, Tutankhamen hunts lions with a *khepesh*. Also used in battle, the curved sword was a design copied by the Egyptians from their Hyksos enemies.

Armour

Soldiers carried **shields** made of wood covered in ox-hide for protection against flying stones, arrows and spears. New Kingdom soldiers had begun to wear leather and cloth bands to protect their chests, as well as a leather cap or a padded cloth helmet on their heads. Princes and generals wore armoured tunics, made by sewing small pieces of bronze onto cloth, and metal helmets. The pharaoh wore a special blue helmet.

Spears

Spears had wooden shafts, on to which metal points were fixed. The throwing spear or javelin had a slender point. The stabbing spear had a much broader blade, like the spears used by hunters to kill big animals, such as lions. Some spears were 2 metres long, and would have been useful to make a barricade, stuck in the sand at an angle to make a 'fence' of sharp points that would keep off an onrushing enemy.

Slinging stones

Probably the oldest of all weapons is the stone. Stone-throwers or **slingers** hurled round stones from a sling or pouch made from a strip of cloth or leather. The sling was whirled around the head and when one end was released the stone went flying off.

This royal dagger and scabbard, made of gold, was among weapons buried alongside the boy-king Tutankhamen. There are only a few specks of rust on the iron blade, after more than three thousand years.

23

Mercenaries

It made little sense to have a huge army of soldiers hanging around in **barracks** when there was no fighting to be done. People were more useful growing food or building pyramids. The families of young men about to be taken for the army would often tell the recruiting official to go to the next village, where they said that men were stronger!

Soldiers' complaints

Like soldiers in every age, Egyptian soldiers liked to complain. Here is part of a text written about 1300 BC, describing the life of a soldier: 'He has many people above him: generals, captains, standard-bearers, commanders … they get their orders from the royal tent and then they shout: "Rouse yourselves! Wake up!" The soldier wakes up after barely an hour's sleep and they keep him busy from dawn till dusk.'

Nubian soldiers were often mercenaries for Egyptian pharaohs. These Nubian archers are models from a pharaoh's tomb.

Dedu the Nubian

Some 'foreigners' rose high. Dedu was a Nubian, who was chosen by the pharaoh Thutmose III to lead the Medjay troops. The Medjay were Nubian soldiers who had fought bravely against the Hyksos invaders. The Nubians became Egypt's national police, and with the title of 'Superintendent of the Western Deserts' (west of the Nile), Dedu led his soldiers across the sands to make sure all the desert peoples obeyed the pharaoh.

Who were the mercenaries?

Many foreign soldiers were happy to put up with this life. They were **mercenaries**, who were ready to fight for Egypt in return for a share in Egypt's wealth.

Foreign soldiers added new fighting skills to the army. There were **Nubian** spearmen, Libyan archers and Sherdens (Shardana) from Sardinia, who fought with long swords. The Sherdens were one of the invaders the Egyptians called '**Sea Peoples**', who came from across the Mediterranean Sea. They were willing to change sides, for money, and were such good fighters that the pharaohs used them as personal **bodyguards**. The Egyptians also hired Greek, Philistine and Hebrew soldiers. **Archaeologists** have found evidence of the military settlements where these foreign troops lived.

Jobs for the mercenaries

Mercenary troops were sent out on desert patrols or to guard frontiers. Some were trusted enough to be royal guards, or to serve as runners and carry messages. Egypt needed extra troops to boost its army, to fight powerful enemies such as the Mitanni (who lived in what is now Iraq) and the **Hittites** (from what is now Turkey).

Forts and sieges

Egyptians had forts as big and strong as many castles built 3000 years later. Some forts had walls 40 metres high and 10 metres thick. Within the walls was a small town. Forts were made of sun-baked mud-brick, the cheapest Egyptian building material, and stone.

Buhen fort

Buhen was one of a chain of forts built along the River Nile. Each one was close enough to be seen from the next, so that soldiers could signal for help if attacked. Buhen was studied by **archaeologists** before it was hidden beneath the waters of Lake Nasser, a lake created in 1964 by the newly built Aswan Dam.

Egyptian forts, such as Buhen, Semna and Mirgissa, were as big as any European castle of the Middle Ages. Buhen probably contained more than 15 million mud bricks. This photo was taken before the waters of Lake Aswan covered the site in 1964.

Over the top

In the 700s BC, a Kushite ruler named Piye (or Piankhi) set out to conquer Egypt. His advance northward brought him to Hermopolis, in Upper Egypt, a city he found 'foul to the nose' (bad-smelling) after five months of siege. To bring a speedy victory, Piye told his men to build an earth bank, with a wooden stockade on top, so high that from its top soldiers could fire over the city walls. Bombarded with stones, spears and arrows, the Egyptians inside Hermopolis soon surrendered.

Built around 1860 BC, Buhen fort was near the border of Egypt and **Nubia**. It stretched for 150 metres along the Nile bank. Inside its twin walls was a small town, with houses set out in a grid system. About 2000 soldiers and around 3000 civilians lived inside the fort. The main wall was about 5 metres thick and 10 metres high, with towers and fortified gateways. Around the main wall was an outer wall, and a water-filled moat 3 metres deep. Enemy soldiers crossing the moat could be fired on by Egyptian troops on the walls, and the enemy would have to climb over both walls to reach the town itself.

In fact, the experts found no evidence of any battle at Buhen, apart from some scorch marks on the mud walls, possibly from a fire. The fort was used as a checkpoint for travellers and traders passing up and down the Nile, and as a repair base for riverboats.

Attacking enemy strongholds

When setting out to capture an enemy town or fort, the Egyptians often began a long **siege**. They surrounded the town to stop food and help getting in, and then they might try to attack it – or simply wait for the enemy to give in. Such sieges might last months or even years – it took 29 years to capture the city of Azotus (Ashdod in modern Israel) in the 600s BC! The Egyptians used **battering rams** to bash down the gates, dug tunnels to weaken the walls and climbed up long ladders to get inside. By the 700s BC, soldiers were building high wooden towers to get into enemy strongholds.

Army on the march

An Egyptian soldier had to be fit, because he walked every step of every journey. When the army left on a campaign, thousands of people and many donkey-loads of supplies went with it.

At the head of each division was its commanding general, and under him were junior officers. With the soldiers went priests, doctors, **scribes**, messengers, armourers (to look after weapons and armour) and grooms (to look after the horses). Caravans of donkeys carried the food supplies.

Organizing the expedition

There are ancient records of ration lists and of factories which made weapons for the army. On one army expedition, we know from the written records that there were three thousand soldiers, and that each man received a daily ration of bread and two pots of water. The soldiers dug **wells** as they marched, leaving guards at each well to make sure they had water for the return journey.

Egyptians in camp, from the tomb paintings of Userhet, Royal Scribe of Amenophis II. At the top an officer speaks to his soldiers, in the middle recruits wait and at the bottom troops have their hair cut and sleep.

Food and fears

Egyptians ate mainly bread and vegetables, with meat or fish as a treat. Soldiers moaned about their 'disgusting' food, and thought wistfully about a good meal at home. They feared being killed, wounded or catching a disease. A soldier lucky enough to come home would be 'worn out, an old man before his time'. However, an inscription says 'if he ran away and deserted, he would be a hunted man and his family would be thrown into jail.'

A large expedition included groups of soldiers from every local district, called a **nome**. Each nome's governor had to supply at least 40 men. This 'nome guard' might have to escort a trade expedition to Nubia, to travel by ship along the Red Sea, or to march as far north as Syria to fight the troublesome **Hittites**.

Making camp

On the march, the soldiers made camp every night. They dug a trench and made a wall with the loose soil. Within this wall, they set up tents made of leather stretched over wooden frames. The biggest tent, in the middle, was the pharaoh's. Close by, in another tent, were statues of the gods carried with the army. Officers had servants to cook dinner and unfold camp beds for the night. Ordinary soldiers, ten to a tent, looked after themselves, eating their meal squatting on the ground. If they were lucky, they drank beer. Officers drank wine (wine jars have been found by **archaeologists**).

Scouts and scribes

Scouts rode on ahead of the army to watch for danger. They were the only Egyptians who regularly rode on horseback. The pharaoh and princes rode in their **chariots**. Scribes also went with the soldiers, to write reports (usually flattering) of the next victory. After a battle, the Egyptians chopped off one hand from each dead enemy. The scribes counted the hands, for the records.

Foreign wars

Egyptian soldiers often fought far away from their homes. Pharaoh Thutmose I (reigned 1493 BC to about 1482 BC) led a force south along the Nile into **Nubia**, to seize gold and to fight the Kushites. Having won that war, the pharaoh turned to the north, to fight the still-troublesome Hyksos. He marched as far east as the Euphrates River in pursuit of the Hyksos army, and invaded Syria to show his power.

Thutmose III goes to war

His grandson Thutmose III (reigned 1479 BC TO 1426 BC) continued these campaigns in the north. Thutmose III was perhaps the greatest of all Egypt's warrior-pharaohs. A skilled horse rider and **archer**, he boasted that none of his generals could outshoot or outride him. Thutmose set out to punish any ruler who defied Egypt by refusing to pay **tribute**. Tribute was a kind of tax (in gold, grain, wood, **slaves** or farm animals) paid by foreign kings and princes to the pharaoh of mighty Egypt.

In Syria and Palestine, to the north, more than 300 unruly princes had joined forces to defy Egypt. Thutmose III set out to teach them a lesson. He began by boldly attacking the city of Megiddo (near the modern city of Haifa in Israel). Normally, Egyptians disliked mountain warfare, but this time their army made a surprise march across mountains. After a **siege** lasting eight months, they captured the city.

Thutmose III was perhaps the greatest of all Egypt's soldier-kings. He became ruler at the age of only ten, and for a time his aunt and step-mother Hatshepsut ruled for him, while Thutmose was trained for the throne.

This map shows how in the 1400s BC, Thutmose III sent his armies to crush Egypt's enemies in the lands the Egyptians called 'Asia', including Palestine, Syria and Mesopotamia. Even Greece, Crete, Cyprus and the **Hittites** sent gifts to Egypt at the peak of its power.

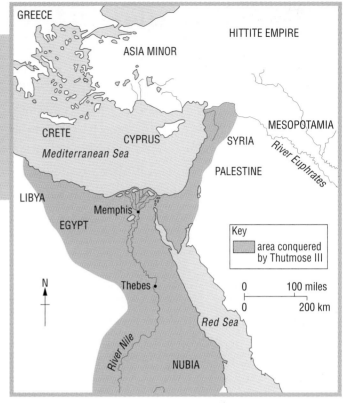

The fruits of victory

Thutmose III then turned east and, in the 33rd year of his reign, invaded the kingdom of Mitanni (in what is now Iraq). Ox-carts trundled collapsible boats across Syria, to carry his soldiers over the Euphrates River. In the battle that followed, the prince of Mitanni fled and many captives were taken. Thutmose returned home in triumph, pausing (it is said) to hunt elephants on the way.

From Egyptian writings, we know that Thutmose III organized and led seventeen campaigns against Egypt's enemies. This warrior-pharaoh built many temples and monuments to celebrate his victories. Conquered princes had to promise to keep the peace and pay their taxes. They were also made to send their sons to Egypt, as **hostages** and to be raised as Egyptians. Timber, cattle, grain and gold poured into Egypt from the defeated kingdoms. The pharaoh's power seemed supreme.

How the Egyptians captured Joppa

Thutmose III captured the town of Joppa (Jaffa, now part of Tel Aviv, Israel) by a trick. He hid 200 soldiers in sacks (one soldier in each sack), and filled 300 more sacks with weapons. His General Tehuti told the townspeople that the Egyptians were giving up, and leaving 500 sacks full of farewell gifts. When the foolish citizens opened the gates, in marched 500 unarmed Egyptians, carrying the bulging sacks. Once inside, they opened the sacks, and out jumped the hidden soldiers. Seizing the weapons, the Egyptians then captured the town!

Keeping the peace

The great soldier-king Thutmose III probably learned much from his aunt and step-mother Hatshepsut, Egypt's most remarkable woman ruler. She seems to have been a much tougher character than his father, her brother Thutmose II. We know that she sent armies south to fight in **Nubia**, and that she also sent a famous military and trade expedition down the Red Sea to the Land of Punt.

Egyptian soldiers return from the Land of Punt, with herbs, plants and trees. Military expeditions opened up new trade routes, as well as providing Egypt with luxuries, such as incense, and exotic animals, such as pet baboons.

An unusual present

Soldiers returning from foreign lands often brought back unusual 'presents'. An officer named Harkhuf came back from Nubia with a 'dancing dwarf', as a gift for the pharaoh Pepi II, a boy of nine years old. Harkhuf sent a letter by messenger to tell the pharaoh about the dwarf. Pepi replied anxiously, telling Harkhuf to take care 'lest the dwarf should fall into the water' during the return trip by boat along the Nile!

Curse the Nubians

Nubia was 'up-country' to an Egyptian soldier. Famed for its gold and its fighting men, Nubia had been a battleground ever since early Egyptian armies had marched south to seize Nubians as **slaves**. Nubian chiefs seldom remained peaceful for long. Egyptian soldiers were regularly sent hurrying along the 'Oasis Road' to punish the Nubians. They would burn their crops and villages, and return with **loot**. Nubian war-chiefs struck back by raiding Egyptian towns and stealing Egyptian cattle. The Egyptians asked the gods to curse the Nubians by writing the names of enemy chiefs on clay figures, which were then ceremonially smashed by a priest.

The expedition to Punt

Hatshepsut's mission to Punt was more peaceful. Punt was a land somewhere in the 'Horn of Africa' (roughly where Sudan, Eritrea and Ethiopia are today). The Egyptians went in great ships. An Egyptian artist created a wall-picture showing the fleet arriving in Punt and being greeted by the local king and his wife, with her donkey. In exchange for beads, knives, beer and wine, the Egyptians loaded their ships with fabulous treasures. The soldiers and sailors came back with gold, living **myrrh** trees, ebony wood, elephant ivory, baboons, cheetahs and greyhounds.

War at sea

For the Egyptians, the River Nile was a vital transport route. There were hardly any roads in Egypt, so many people were as skilled in sailing a boat as they were in driving a donkey.

Going to sea

The Egyptians were the first people to build seagoing boats. The oldest known pictures of boats, found in Egypt, are at least 6000 years old.

Most Egyptian boats were made from bundles of **papyrus** reeds, but some ships were made from wood. Remains of a large boat were found in 1954 near the Pyramid of Khufu at Giza. It was made of cedar wood, probably from Lebanon, a land famous for its cedar trees. Fleets of as many as 40 ships went to Lebanon to collect timber.

Found in 1224 pieces, the boat at Giza has been reconstructed. The thin oars would have propelled it through the water – some other boats were powered by wind and sail.

Rowing into battle

Rowing was hard work. All the oarsmen had to row in time to propel the boat towards the enemy. Writing on a wall painting in a tomb from the 6th **Dynasty** shows two oarsmen. One is saying: 'Row harder, comrade! Faster!' The other wearily replies: 'I am rowing, but everyone keeps telling me to row harder'.

The biggest ships were about 50 metres long and carried over 100 men. Because they had no keel (a length of wood acting as the ship's stiffening 'backbone'), they tended to sag at either end. To stop this, Egyptian shipbuilders stretched a tight rope from end to end. A **scribe** called Ineri wrote about giant barges 120 **cubits** long (about 60 metres), used to carry huge stone **obelisks**.

Egyptian sea power

About 2500 BC, Pharaoh Sahure sent eight Egyptian ships to attack Syria and bring back prisoners. Fragments of a stone **relief** show one of these ships. It has a mast, made from two poles fastened at the top, which could have been folded down when not needed. Sailors used paddles or oars to drive the ship along when there was no wind.

A later picture shows a sea battle between Egyptian ships and those of the **Sea Peoples**. It took place during the time of Ramses III, when the Egyptian navy saved Egypt from disaster. The pharaoh's vessels, with proud names, such as 'Falcon Ship', rowed into battle in squadrons (groups of ships) under the overall command of an admiral.

What a sea battle was like

Each warship carried a crew of oarsmen and about 200 soldiers. Battle began with furious exchanges of arrows, spears and stones, as each steersman tried to move his ship close to an enemy vessel. Sailors hurled pots of burning oil to set fire to wooden ships and sails. As ships crashed together, Egyptian soldiers leapt on to the enemy craft, fighting with clubs, axes and swords. In the later stages of Egypt's history, Egyptian warships had **catapults** to fling stones or balls of blazing tar at the enemy.

The general

Generals held great power in Egypt, and some became pharaohs. Not all generals were Egyptians. Urhiya, a general under Seti I (1290 BC to 1279 BC), came from the Palestine-Syria region, but fought loyally for Egypt. Soldiers gained supreme power usually when pharaohs were young or weak. After the death of Tutankhamen, who had no children to reign after him, an old man named Ay ruled for four years. When Ay died, General Horemheb took his place as pharaoh.

Horemheb's rise to power

Horemheb may have come from Heracleopolis, an important city in central Egypt, though not much is known about his early life. He made his name as an army officer during the reign of Amenhotep III, when the pharaoh was fighting rebels in **Nubia**. Horemheb must have done well in these wars, because the next pharaoh, Akhenaten, made him Great Commander of the Army.

When Horemheb became pharaoh, he supported Egypt's old gods. This statue shows him with the falcon-headed god Horus. He was the last pharaoh of the 18th Dynasty.

A general's dirty trick

A clever general did not shrink from an unfair trick to outwit an enemy. Tehuti was Pharaoh Thutmose III's best general. During the **siege** of Joppa (described on page 31) he invited the prince of Joppa to a feast. The prince drank too much wine and drunkenly asked if he might see the pharaoh's war-club. Tehuti fetched it, hit the prince on the head, knocked him out and had him bound in chains!

Horemheb must have hated Akhenaten's reign. The pharaoh was more interested in his new sun god religion than in the army. The old gods were set aside. When the boy-pharaoh Tutankhamen was made pharaoh in 1333 BC, Horemheb became 'Pharaoh's Deputy', the second most powerful man in Egypt. He led an army north into Lebanon and Palestine to fight the **Hittites** and the Nubians again. Tomb-pictures show Tutankhamen gaining the glory for more victories, but Horemheb had won the battles.

The general becomes pharaoh

When he made himself pharaoh, in about 1319 BC, Horemheb destroyed all traces of the four rulers before him – Ay, Tutankhamen, Smenkhare and Akhenaten. Inscriptions were written to make it look as if he came straight after Amenhotep, the last great soldier-pharaoh. Such 'rewriting of history' was common in ancient Egypt, when a new ruler was anxious to show himself in the best possible light.

Horemheb picked soldiers to run his government, and to be priests. He reigned for almost 30 years. To make sure that no general could challenge him, Horemheb split the army into two separate commands, north and south. He chose his chief minister (or vizier) to be his successor. This ruler, Ramses I, was the founder of the 19th **Dynasty**, a line of great soldier-pharaohs.

Last of the warrior-pharaohs

The last great warrior-pharaohs were Seti I, Ramses II and Ramses III. They faced an enemy – the **Hittites** – who were the first people to make iron weapons and were therefore better armed than themselves. Ramses II fought the Hittites at a famous battle in 1275 BC at Kadesh, close to the Orontes River in Syria.

The battle of Kadesh

Ramses II marched into Syria with an army of four divisions, each (as was the custom) named after a god: Amen, Re, Ptah and Setekh. So he had about 20,000 men in all. The Hittite king Muwatallis cunningly hid his army behind the mound on which the city of Kadesh was built. Thinking the enemy had withdrawn, Ramses hurried towards Kadesh and made camp. Too late, he found out his mistake.

Hundreds of Hittite **chariots** charged out from hiding, scattering two Egyptian divisions. According to the Egyptians, Ramses led his **bodyguard** in a desperate charge to halt the Hittites, who **looted** the Egyptian camp before being driven off by fresh Egyptian troops. The Egyptians claimed the victory, but neither side really won.

Victorious pharaohs received gifts from vanquished foreign rulers. This tomb painting (about 1450 BC) shows Nubians and Minoans (from Crete) with a selection of gifts including elephant tusks, monkeys and a giraffe.

Ramses' heroism was exaggerated in many inscriptions in Egyptian temples. A Hittite version, found at the ancient town of Boghazkoy, is less flattering about Ramses' part in the battle. The two sides made peace and Ramses married a Hittite princess. Ramses II's son Merneptah showed his goodwill by sending food to the Hittites during a famine.

Ramses fights the Sea Peoples

The last winning pharaoh was Ramses III, who fought off the invaders called **Sea Peoples** by the Egyptians. Little is known about these seafaring warriors from across the Mediterranean Sea, who defeated the Hittites and Syrians before turning on Egypt.

Ramses fought the Sea Peoples on land in Palestine and at sea in the channels of the Nile Delta (where the Nile met the sea). These were waters his sailors knew well and 'the net was made ready', an Egyptian historian wrote, 'ready to ensnare them'. In Ramses III's temple at Medinet Habu there is a stone-carved picture of the sea battle.

The Egyptians had improved their warships, raising the sides to keep off waves, enemy spears and arrows. They smashed into enemy vessels with their metal-tipped **battering rams**. The defeated Sea Peoples turned away to settle elsewhere. Victory saved Egypt and prisoners were branded with the pharaoh's name and settled in military camps. Ramses III was proud of winning peace for Egypt. 'I planted the whole land with leafy trees, and let the people sit in their shade', he declared.

Who were the Sea Peoples?

Except that they were aggressive sea-fighters, very little else is known about the Sea Peoples. Egyptian history records two wars: first under Pharaoh Merneptah and the second under Ramses III. The Egyptians named the Sea Peoples: Ekwesh (possibly Greeks), Luka (possibly from what is now Turkey) and Teresh (perhaps the ancestors of the Etruscans of Italy). There were also the Sherden (Sardinians) and Peleset (Philistines, originally from Crete).

Egypt invaded

After Ramses III, Egypt had a number of weak pharaohs, none of whom were great soldiers. The Egyptian army was still large. In about 930 BC, Pharaoh Sheshonk I is recorded as attacking Jerusalem with more than 1200 **chariots** and over 60,000 horsemen. Such huge numbers, however, are almost certainly an exaggeration!

Foreign pharaohs and new enemies

Once united, Egypt now broke up, as rival rulers fought for control. This disunity made it easier for a strong outsider to take over. One such foreign pharaoh was Piye (or Piankhi), king of Kush (in what is now Sudan). In the 700s BC, he and his brother defeated Libyan princes and others to set up the 25th **Dynasty**.

For the rest of its history, Egypt faced attack from outside. The army fought in vain to keep out the Assyrians, fierce rulers of an **empire** in what is now Syria and Iraq.

Ptolemy Soter ruled Egypt from 323 to 285 BC. He made Egypt the strongest sea power in the Mediterranean, and founded a ruling family that reigned for almost 300 years.

Alexander's general

One of Alexander the Great's best generals was another Macedonian, Ptolemy Soter ('Saviour'). He became Alexander's personal **bodyguard** and helped to win the battles that made Alexander the most famous conqueror in history. After Alexander died in 323 BC, his generals split his empire between them. Ptolemy became ruler of Egypt and named himself its pharaoh in 305 BC.

The Assyrians massed the biggest armies yet seen, up to 120,000 soldiers. They wore metal armour, fired powerful bows from behind basketwork **shields** and rode in heavy armoured chariots. No town was safe against their **siege** engines, massive towers on wheels, with swinging **battering rams** to smash down walls. Tales of Assyrian ferocity terrified their enemies.

Conquerors come and go

The Assyrian king Sennacherib (704 BC to 680 BC) defeated Egypt's army in Palestine. His successors, Esarhaddon and Assurbanipal, had conquered Egypt by 664 BC.

After the Assyrians, other conquerors came and went in their turn. In the 500s BC, the Persian king Cambyses made Egypt a province of the Persian Empire. In 332 BC came Alexander the Great and after him a line of Greek pharaohs, the Ptolemies. The last of the Ptolemies was Queen Cleopatra. She killed herself in 30 BC after she and her ally, the Roman general Mark Antony, lost the sea battle of Actium against the Roman navy.

This defeat ended Egypt's independence, as it became part of the Roman Empire. Yet so ancient was Egypt's history, and so strong its traditions, that much of its unique culture survived.

Buried history

We know about the ancient Egyptians from their tombs, their temples and palaces, and their **monuments**. The pharaohs of Egypt were determined to record their battles and victories for later generations, in writings and pictures. They set up stone pillars, known as *stelae*, to record their triumphs. The Egyptians were painstaking record-keepers and their **scribes** wrote lists of victories, including the numbers of enemy soldiers killed and captured.

Tomb discoveries

The Egyptians buried their pharaohs in tombs, some in pyramids and others in rock tombs in the Valley of the Kings. Astounding finds came from the tomb of Tutankhamen, opened in 1922 by a British **archaeologist** named Howard Carter. Most royal tombs had been robbed long ago, but Tutankhamen was an unimportant ruler whose grave had been overlooked. Inside, Carter found 'wonderful things' – jewels, gold, vases, statues, **chariots** and weapons and, in its gold coffin, the **mummy** of Tutankhamen himself.

Tutankhamen was not a warrior-leader like Ramses II, who decorated temple walls with scenes of his battles and triumphs. Yet the boy-pharaoh's treasures are the finest recovered from an Egyptian royal tomb, and a rich source of historical evidence.

Later kings of Egypt were buried in tombs here, in the Valley of the Kings. Each tomb contained treasure for the pharaoh's use in the afterlife, but most tombs were broken into and emptied by robbers.

What archaeologists look for

Such finds are very rare. Most of what we know comes from scraps of evidence, from towns, forts and military camps that have been excavated by archaeologists. From such sites, we can build up a picture of how Egyptian soldiers lived, what their weapons were like, what they ate, and so on. Finds include remains of clothing, armour, tools and weapons. Occasionally, through a fragment of writing or a faded picture, we come face to face with a long-dead Egyptian, telling us part of his or her own story.

This evidence helps us picture life in ancient Egypt, recalling the warriors and weapons of a once-mighty empire. In this book we have been able to explore the times of an Egyptian warrior, to learn how he lived and fought, on land and at sea. For 3000 years, Egypt's warriors defended their home, the rich green land beside the mighty River Nile.

This sculpted image shows Egyptian officials leading off bearded prisoners. It comes from the tomb of Horemheb. Pictures like this give us evidence of how Egyptian warfare was conducted.

The Rosetta Stone

The oldest Egyptian writings are in **hieroglyphics**, or picture-signs. Later ones are in other languages, such as Greek. How to read hieroglyphic writing was forgotten, until the discovery in AD 1799 of the Rosetta Stone. This black stone, found half-buried in mud near Rosetta in northern Egypt, had the same inscription in three forms of writing: hieroglyphics, an abbreviated form (called demotic) and Greek. It was the key to breaking the hieroglyphic code. Scholars were able to translate the signs and read Egyptian texts for the first time.

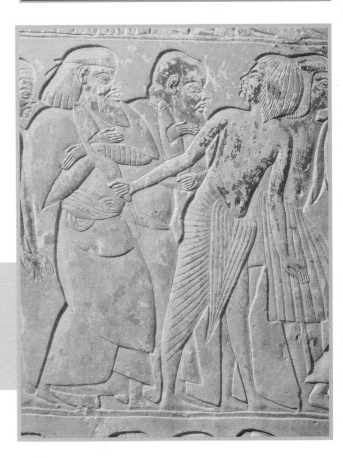

Timeline

All dates are BC. Pharaoh's dates refer to reigns.
All dates are approximate as they vary from source to source.

Before 5000
Early settlers farmed and built towns along the Nile.

About 3000
Menes unites Lower and Upper Egypt. **Dynasties** (ruling families) 1, 2 and 3.

2575 to 2130 The Old Kingdom
Great Pyramids are built at Giza. Dynasties 4 to 8.
Trading expeditions, war with Libyans.
Pepi I (c.2325 to c.2150) and his official Weni.

2130 to 1938 First Intermediate Period
A time of weak rulers. Dynasties 9, 10 and 11.

1938 to 1600 Middle Kingdom
Power of pharaohs is restored. Dynasties 12 and 13.
Wars with **Nubians** in the south. Sesostris III builds new forts.

1630 to 1540 Second Intermediate Period
Dynasties 14 to 17. Invasion of Hyksos. Egyptians meet first **chariots**.

1539 to 1075 New Kingdom
Dynasties 18 to 20. Egypt's power at its height. Ahmose I (1539 to 1514) leads its first full-time army.
Rulers at this time include: Amenhotep II, the **archer**-pharaoh (1426 to 1400); Thutmose I (1493 until about 1482); Thutmose III (1479 to 1426); Hatshepsut (died about 1458), who sends a famous expedition to the Land of Punt; Amenhotep III (1390 to 1353) leads army to victories.
Seti I (1290 to 1279) fights **Hittites**.
Ramses II (1279 to 1213) known as Ramses the Great.
Battle of Kadesh fought in 1275 between Egyptians and Hittites.
Ramses III (1187 to 1156) drives off invaders known as the **Sea Peoples**.

1075 to 665 Third Intermediate Period

Dynasties 21 to 25. Pharaohs of Libyan heritage rule (dynasties 21 to 23).
Dynasty 25 were Kushite rulers.

664 to 332 Late period, a time of foreign rule

Dynasties 26 to 30. Local rulers struggle for power. Dynasty 27 were
Persian kings who did not live in Egypt but styled themselves as pharaohs.
Dynasties 28 to 30 were native rulers.
332 Alexander the Great from Greece conquers the country.
New dynasty, under Ptolemy, a Greek, is founded in 305.
47 Cleopatra rules Egypt.
31 Defeat by Roman fleet at sea battle of Actium ends Egypt's power.
Romans make Egypt a Roman province.

Sources and further reading

Sources

Going to War in Ancient Egypt, Anne Millard
(Franklin Watts, 2001)

Myths and Legends of Egypt, Lewis Spence
(Studio Editions, 1994)

Technology in the Time of Ancient Egypt, Judith Crosher
(Wayland, 1997)

The British Museum Book of Ancient Egypt, eds. Quirke and Spencer
(British Museum Press, 1992)

Further reading

How Would You Survive as an Ancient Egyptian? Jacqueline Morley
(Franklin Watts, 1999)

Legacies from Ancient Egypt, Anita Ganeri
(Belitha Press, 1999)

The Life and World of Tutankhamen, Brian Williams
(Heinemann Library, 2002)

Glossary

archaeologist person who finds out about the past by looking for the remains of buildings and other objects, often beneath the ground

archer soldier who fires arrows from a bow

barracks building where soldiers live

battering ram heavy tree trunk with metal tip for bashing down fort gates and city walls

Bedouins wandering people of the desert

bodyguard soldiers who protect a ruler

bronze metal made by mixing melted copper and tin, used in ancient times for tools and weapons

catapult machine for throwing rocks or other missiles, worked by twisted ropes or weights

cavalry soldiers on horseback

chariot light cart with two wheels, pulled by horses

civilization society with its own rules and an advanced way of life

composite made of more than one material

conscripts people drafted or ordered to serve in the army

copper soft metal used to make tools and weapons

cubit Egyptian unit of measurement (based on length from fingertip to elbow)

dynasty ruling family. The first Egyptian historian Manetho listed 30 dynasties of pharaohs.

empire lands and peoples ruled by a strong power or ruler

garrison group of soldiers who guard a fort or army base

helmet warrior's hat, made from padded cloth, leather or metal, and worn to protect the head

hieroglyphs Egyptian picture-writing, the name means 'sacred writing' in Greek

Hittite warlike people who lived in what is now Turkey and invented tools made of iron

hostage someone held prisoner to make sure his or her friends do what the captors demand

infantry foot-soldiers

kilt short skirt-like garment

linen cloth made from the woven fibres of the flax plant

litter seat with poles, in which rich people were carried about

loot goods taken from a defeated enemy

mercenaries soldiers who hire themselves out to fight for pay

monument building or statue in memory of a famous person or event

mummy body of a dead person specially treated to stop it decaying

myrrh tree with resin (sap) used to make sweet-smelling perfumes

noble person of high rank, next in social hierarchy after the pharaoh

nomad person who has no settled home, but wanders

nomarch governor of a local district (nome) working for the pharaoh

nome one of 42 local districts in Egypt

Nubia land to the south of Egypt, in what is now Sudan; part of the Egyptian empire

obelisk tall stone monument, four-sided with a pointed top

papyrus reed with many uses, including making a kind of paper

quiver pouch for carrying arrows

relief picture cut into stone, so that figures stand out

sacrifice offering to a god

scout soldier sent ahead of an army to spy out the land

scribe person trained to write

Sea Peoples groups of seafaring peoples from the eastern Mediterranean who attacked Hittites, Syrians and Egyptians

shield hand-held guard, made from wood, animal skin or metal, to protect a soldier from enemy blows

sickle curved tool for cutting wheat and other cereal crops

siege attack on a defended town when town is cut off from outside help

slave person who is not free, but has to work for an owner

slinger soldier who hurls stones

standard pole with a special badge or symbol on top, carried by soldiers

tribute gifts handed over by people to their rulers

veteran person who has much experience

well hole dug to reach underground water

Index

Titles in the *Ancient Egyptian* series include:

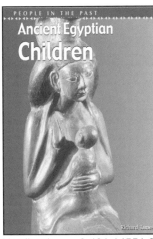

Hardback   0 431 14551 2

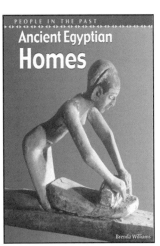

Hardback   0 431 14581 4

Hardback   0 431 14583 0

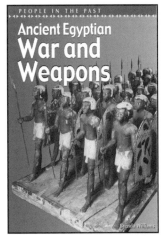

Hardback   0 431 14580 6

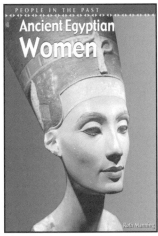

Hardback   0 431 14582 2

Find out about the other titles in this series on our website www.heinemann.co.uk/library